THE
perfect
blending
COOKBOOK

DEVELOPED BY
WILLIAMS
SONOMA
TEST KITCHEN

Photographs Maren Caruso

weldon**owen**

Contents

Welcome to Power Blending

The Vitamix® Professional Series™ blender is a powerful kitchen appliance that will change the way you cook and prepare food. The engine makes the blades turn so fast that they can process foods in an instant. We use it in the Williams-Sonoma Test Kitchen to blend everything from piping hot soups to freezing cold milk shakes. This blender crushes ice and blends ingredients into creamy, smooth concoctions in under 1 minute and also warms liquids like sauces and soups through friction when left on for 5 minutes or longer.

Discover how easy it is to prepare salad dressings, smoothies, soups, sauces, marinades, and more in the Vitamix blender. Use this amazing appliance to instantly purée just about anything into a smooth texture and to mince, chop, crush, and shred ingredients. You can make everything from fresh pico de gallo and fruit chutney to apple muffin batter and graham cracker crusts.

On the pages that follow, you'll find a primer on how to use the Vitamix blender to prepare a variety of recipes using an array of ingredients. More than 30 recipes are featured, from breakfast to dinner, snacks to dessert. Try Crepes with Mixed Berry Compote & Whipped Cream (page 16) for a celebratory brunch; fresh Tossed Salad with Green Goddess Dressing (page 32) for a light lunch with friends; the comforting Vegetable Lasagne with Roasted Tomato Sauce (page 33) for a family-friendly meal; or rich Bittersweet Chocolate Pudding (page 50) for a decadent dessert. Any way you blend it, you're sure to make the most out of your Vitamix blender with this companion cookbook.

Power Blender Primer

Getting to know your Vitamix® Professional Series™ blender will enable you to take full advantage of all that it can do, from blending and chopping to puréeing and warming soups.

- Place your blender on a stable work surface, then plug the unit into a wall outlet.

- The control panel varies slightly from machine to machine, but all of them have a power switch and speed controls. Professional Series models also feature a variable speed-control dial and some have a pulse switch, and preprogrammed settings.

- The capacity of the blender container can vary depending on the model. Measurements are marked on the outside of the container in cups, ounces, and milliliters.

- The standard blender container is the wet blade container, which pulls food down to blend it smoothly.

- An optional secondary container, the dry blade container, is ideal for grinding flours, grains, and coffee and for kneading dough. It is designed to force food up into the container to ensure it doesn't clump. (The dry blade container is not standard with the Vitamix® Professional Series™ blender and can be purchased separately.)

- Your blender is designed to work continuously, so you don't need to stop and scrape down the sides as with other blenders or food processors.

- The blender comes with a sturdy tamper, which allows you to push ingredients towards the blender blades and prevent air pockets from forming—handy when blending thick mixtures. The tamper is designed to be used with the lid in place and will not hit the blade, as long as you use the tamper that comes with your specific machine.

Lid
with a removable plug

Container
includes the
blade assembly

Tamper
allows you
to push food
toward the
blades

Powerful engine
housed in the base

Vitamix

Control panel
includes speed-control dial
and pulse switch

Power Blender Tips & Tricks

Preparing a variety of recipes in the Vitamix® Professional Series™ blender is a snap. These tips for using and caring for your appliance will help you maximize your blending experience.

Cutting up & peeling ingredients

For fruits and vegetables that will be puréed, cut them into 2- or 3-inch chunks before placing in the blender. In general, cut long vegetables like carrots, celery, cucumbers, and green onions into thirds. If the food has a tender skin, you don't have to peel it; the blender purées so well that you won't know the peel is there, but you will get the extra nutrition and fiber from the skin.

Puréeing ingredients to a smooth consistency

Add the ingredients to the blender container and start at speed 1, then gradually increase to the machine's highest speed. For frozen desserts, run for 45 seconds; for smoothies, run for 45–60 seconds; and for general puréeing, run for 1 minute.

Pulsing

Use this method when you want a partially smooth consistency with some texture remaining. Select the desired speed and then turn the machine on and off using the pulse switch, repeating until the desired consistency is reached.

Dry chopping

Use this method with nuts, cheese, or firm vegetables, such as carrots, when they will be incorporated into a dish. With the blades running on a low speed, drop pieces of the ingredient into the container. This will take only a few seconds and the results will vary in size and shape. For a more precise chop, use the wet chop method.

Wet chopping

Use this method for slicing or shredding vegetables and anytime you need a uniform chop. Put large pieces of the food in the blender container and add enough water so that the food floats above the blades (this helps pull the food down into the blades for a consistent cut). Pulse just until the food is shredded; it will happen very quickly. Drain well and use as directed.

Heating soups

Add the ingredients to the blender container and start at speed 1, then gradually increase to the machine's highest speed and run for 5-6 minutes.

Cleanup

A blender is so easy to clean—it actually cleans itself! Just fill the container half full with warm water and add 1 or 2 drops of dish soap. Put the lid, including the plug, in place tightly. Start at speed 1, then gradually increase to the machine's highest speed and run for 30-60 seconds. Rinse the container, and you are done. Do not put the container or the lid in the dishwasher, which could damage them.

When you are done

Always set the speed dial back to 1 after blending. That way, the machine will be at the right speed the next time you start it.

What can be power blended?

A wide range of foods—from savory to sweet, frozen to hot—can be prepared in the Power Blender:

- sauces & salsas
- dressings & marinades
- soups
- batters & doughs
- savory & sweet crusts
- egg dishes
- smoothies
- dips
- frozen desserts
- coleslaws
- blended drinks
- chutneys & compotes

Spiced Apple Muffins with Honey Butter

These delicious muffins are the perfect treat anytime, from a cozy weekend breakfast or afternoon coffee to an on-the-go snack. The honey butter will keep in the refrigerator for several weeks.

Preheat the oven to 375°F. Make the streusel and honey butter and set aside. Grease and flour 12 standard muffin cups or line with paper liners.

In a large bowl, whisk together the flour, cinnamon, allspice, baking powder, baking soda, and salt. Set aside.

In the blender, combine the apple, melted butter, buttermilk, and sugar. Blend, starting at 1 and slowly working up to 10, until the apple is puréed and the mixture is well combined, 2–3 minutes. It's okay if there are a few lumps of apple. Add the egg and blend, starting at 1 and slowly working up to 10, until combined, 15–20 seconds.

Add the apple mixture to the flour mixture and gently stir until fully combined. Let the batter rest for 5–10 minutes. Divide the batter among the prepared muffin cups and crumble the frozen streusel on top.

Bake until the muffins are golden brown and a toothpick inserted into the center comes out clean, 20–25 minutes. Let the muffins cool in the pan on a wire rack for 10 minutes, then turn them out onto the rack and let cool completely. Serve the muffins with the honey butter.

MAKES 12 MUFFINS

1 recipe Streusel (page 59)

1 recipe Honey Butter (page 58)

½ cup plus 2 tablespoons unsalted butter, melted, plus more for greasing

2 cups all-purpose flour, plus more for dusting

2 teaspoons ground cinnamon

1 teaspoon ground allspice

1 teaspoon baking powder

1 teaspoon baking soda

1 teaspoon kosher salt

1 apple, cored and quartered

1 cup buttermilk

¾ cup sugar

1 large egg

Skip the streusel for a quick and tasty muffin that can be made from start to finish in under 1 hour.

Crepes with Mixed Berry Compote & Whipped Cream

The key to these delicate, lacy crepes is to blend the batter until completely smooth. Served with a warm berry compote and sweetened whipped cream, these make an impressive brunch dish.

To make the crepes, in the blender, combine the flour, salt, the eggs, and milk. Blend, starting at 1 and slowly working up to 10, until well combined and smooth, about 30 seconds. Let the batter stand at room temperature for 15 minutes or store in an airtight container in the refrigerator overnight. Wash and dry the blender container. Make the berry compote.

To make the whipped cream, in the blender, combine the cream, sugar, and vanilla bean seeds (if using). Blend, starting at 1 and slowly working up to 10, until whipped cream forms, about 30 seconds.

To cook the crepes, place a small nonstick frying pan over medium-high heat and coat with nonstick cooking spray. Gently stir the batter and pour ¼ cup of it into the pan, lifting and tilting the pan to spread the batter to the edges. Return the pan to the heat and cook until the crepe is golden underneath, about 2 minutes. Using a spatula, flip the crepe and cook until the other side is golden brown, 1–2 minutes longer. Transfer to a plate and cover with a clean dish towel. Repeat to cook the remaining batter.

Cover half of each crepe with berry compote and roll, then top with whipped cream. Serve warm.

SERVES 4

For the crepes

1 cup all-purpose flour

½ teaspoon kosher salt

2 large eggs

1½ cups whole milk

1 recipe Berry Compote (page 56)

For the whipped cream

2 cups heavy cream

½ cup sugar

½ vanilla bean, split and seeds scraped (optional)

Nonstick cooking spray

Spinach & Tomato Frittata

This frittata recipe is easy to customize—use your favorite vegetables, meat, or cheese, and scale quantities up or down depending on the size of your pan. It's a great make-ahead dish; refrigerate overnight, then reheat in a 375°F oven.

Place a rack in the upper third of the oven and preheat to 375°F.

In the blender, combine the spinach and tomatoes. With the speed on 1, pulse until well chopped, about 20 seconds. Transfer to a bowl. In the blender, combine the eggs, milk, a pinch of salt, and a few grindings of pepper. With the speed on 1, pulse just until mixed, about 10 seconds. Set aside.

In an ovenproof 8- to 10-inch nonstick frying pan over medium-high heat, warm 1 tablespoon of the oil. Add the sausage, if using, and cook, stirring, until browned and cooked through, 4–6 minutes. Transfer to a small bowl. Add the spinach mixture to the pan and cook, stirring frequently, until wilted, 2–3 minutes. Season with salt and pepper. Drain in a colander.

In the same pan over medium heat, warm the remaining 1 tablespoon oil. Return the sausage, if using, and the spinach mixture to the pan and stir in the egg mixture. Cook until the edges of the frittata are just set, about 2 minutes. Transfer the pan to the oven and cook until the frittata is golden brown and set in the center, 10–15 minutes. Invert the frittata onto a cutting board. Let cool slightly, then cut into wedges. Garnish with goat cheese, if using, and serve warm.

SERVES 4–6

2 cups spinach

2 tomatoes, quartered

8 large eggs

½ cup whole milk

Kosher salt and freshly ground pepper

2 tablespoons extra-virgin olive oil

4 oz Italian sausage, crumbled (optional)

Crumbled fresh goat cheese, for garnish (optional)

Serve these for brunch and let guests select toppings and assemble their own acai bowls.

Acai Bowl

A grapelike fruit native to South America, acai has been heralded for its antioxidants and superfood health benefits. Acai can be found in individual-sized packets in the frozen food section of supermarkets.

Run the frozen acai packets under warm water for 10 seconds, then open the packets. In the blender, combine the acai, orange juice, and banana. Blend, starting at 1 and slowly working up to 10, until smooth, 15–20 seconds.

Pour the acai mixture into bowls and garnish with the desired toppings. Serve right away.

SERVES 2

2 packets (3½ oz each) frozen acai

½ cup fresh orange juice

1 banana, cut into thirds

Granola, dried coconut, fresh berries (such as strawberries, blueberries, and blackberries), sliced banana, and nuts (such as toasted slivered almonds or walnuts), for serving

Mango-Melon Smoothie

A hint of cardamom provides an aromatic twist to this summery drink. Adjust the amount of honey depending on the sweetness of the melon.

In the blender, combine the orange juice, yogurt, cardamom, cantaloupe, mango, and honey. Blend, starting at 1 and slowly working up to 10, until smooth, about 30 seconds. Serve right away.

SERVES 2

½ cup fresh orange juice

1 cup plain full-fat yogurt

¼ teaspoon ground cardamom

1½ cups diced cantaloupe

1½ cups frozen mango chunks

1–2 tablespoons honey

Kale, Spinach & Apple Smoothie

A host of green fruits and vegetables makes this nutrition-packed smoothie ideal for a healthy breakfast or between-meal pick-me-up.

In the blender, combine the kale, spinach, grapes, cucumber, apple, and ice. Blend, starting at 1 and slowly working up to 10, until smooth, about 30 seconds. Serve right away.

SERVES 2

5 Tuscan kale leaves, stemmed and leaves roughly torn

½ cup packed baby spinach

1 cup seedless green grapes

½ cup peeled, seeded, and diced cucumber

1 green apple, peeled, cored, and quartered

1 cup ice cubes

Chocolate-Hazelnut Spread

This spread is easy to make at home in a Vitamix blender. It's great for filling crepes, spreading on toast, or eating from a spoon! You can also use extra-dark chocolate chips for a more intense flavor.

Preheat the oven to 350°F.

Spread the hazelnuts in a single layer on a baking sheet and toast in the oven until golden brown, about 10 minutes. Let the nuts cool in a kitchen towel, then gently rub off most of the skin.

Fill a saucepan with water to a depth of 2–3 inches and heat over low heat until it barely simmers. In a heatproof bowl, combine the chocolate chips and honey. Place the bowl over but not touching the simmering water and heat, stirring occasionally, until the chocolate is melted. Remove the bowl from the pan and stir in the milk and confectioners' sugar until blended. Let cool slightly.

Put the hazelnuts in the blender. Blend, starting at 1 and slowly working up to 10, until liquefied, about 1 minute. Add the oil, salt, and vanilla and blend, starting at 1 and slowly working up to 10, until combined, about 15 seconds. Add the chocolate mixture and blend, starting at 1 and slowly working up to 10, until combined, about 30 seconds, using the tamper as needed to push down the ingredients.

For a smoother consistency, strain the spread through a fine-mesh sieve. The mixture will thicken as it cools. Store in an airtight container in the refrigerator for up to 1 week.

MAKES ABOUT 2 CUPS

1 cup hazelnuts

½ cup semisweet chocolate chips

½ cup milk-chocolate chips

3 tablespoons honey

½ cup whole milk

1 tablespoon confectioners' sugar

2 tablespoons vegetable oil

2 teaspoons kosher salt

1 teaspoon vanilla extract

Roasted Garlic & Herb Dip

When roasted, garlic becomes golden and buttery soft, with a delicate nutty flavor. Here, the roasted cloves are blended into a dip that is enhanced with a medley of fresh herbs.

Preheat the oven to 400°F.

Cut off the tops of the garlic heads and rub the cut surface with the oil. Put the garlic cut side up on a baking sheet. Arrange the rosemary and thyme sprigs on or around the garlic. Cover the garlic with aluminum foil. Roast until the garlic cloves are soft and lightly browned, about 1¼ hours. Let cool completely.

Squeeze the pulp from the garlic cloves into the blender (discard the herb sprigs). Add the sour cream, mayonnaise, chopped rosemary, chopped thyme, parsley, lemon juice, Worcestershire sauce, 1½ teaspoons salt, and a few grindings of pepper. Blend, starting at 1 and slowly working up to 10, until creamy, 1–2 minutes.

Transfer the dip to a bowl, cover with plastic wrap, and refrigerate for at least 30 minutes or up to 1 week. Serve with potato chips.

MAKES ABOUT 3 CUPS

4 heads garlic

2 tablespoons olive oil

1 fresh rosemary sprig, plus 1½ tablespoons chopped fresh rosemary

1 fresh thyme sprig, plus 1½ tablespoons chopped fresh thyme

1½ cups sour cream

6 tablespoons mayonnaise

3 tablespoons chopped fresh flat-leaf parsley

2 teaspoons fresh lemon juice

¾ teaspoon Worcestershire sauce

Kosher salt and freshly ground pepper

Potato chips, for serving

Vary the flavor by swapping the pepper for 1 large roasted, peeled golden or red beet.

Roasted Red Bell Pepper Hummus

In this fresh take on classic hummus, roasted red bell pepper is blended with the chickpeas to create a dip with bright color and smoky flavor. You can use jarred roasted bell peppers or roast your own for this recipe.

Place an oven rack in the upper portion of the oven and preheat the broiler. Put the bell pepper on a rimmed baking sheet lined with aluminium foil. Place the baking sheet in the oven and broil, turning the bell pepper as needed with tongs, until charred on all sides, about 15 minutes. Transfer the bell pepper to a paper bag and close the bag loosely. When the bell pepper is cool, remove from the bag and use your fingers to peel and rub away the charred skin. Cut off the stem and remove the seeds.

In the blender, combine the bell pepper, chickpeas, garlic, lemon juice, tahini, 1 teaspoon of the paprika, and the cumin. With the speed on 2, pulse until the mixture just comes together, about 1 minute. With the blender running on 4, add the oil through the pour spout in a slow, steady stream and blend until incorporated, about 2 minutes. Adjust the seasoning with salt.

Transfer the hummus to a bowl and sprinkle with the remaining 1 teaspoon paprika. (The dip can be covered and refrigerated for up to 1 week.) Serve with pita bread or pita chips and crudités.

MAKES ABOUT 3 CUPS

1 red bell pepper, or 6 ounces store-bought roasted red bell peppers, roughly chopped

2 cans (15 oz each) chickpeas, drained and rinsed

2 cloves garlic, minced

2 tablespoons fresh lemon juice

¼ cup tahini

2 teaspoons smoked sweet paprika

¼ teaspoon ground toasted cumin seeds

¼ cup olive oil

Kosher salt

Pita bread or pita chips and crudités, such as bell peppers, carrots, cucumber, endive, and radishes, for serving

Chicken & Cheese Enchiladas

These enchiladas are a great way to use up leftover roast chicken. If you don't have any on hand, poach 1½ lb skinless, boneless breasts and shred with 2 forks. Serve with a side of pico de gallo (page 29).

Preheat the oven to 350°F. Lightly grease a 9-by-13-inch baking dish. Make the enchilada sauce.

In a large nonstick sauté pan over medium-high heat, warm the oil. Add the spinach and ¼ cup water and cook until the spinach is wilted, about 2 minutes. Let cool, drain, then coarsely chop. In the same pan over medium-high heat, combine the onion and garlic and season with salt and pepper. Cook, stirring occasionally, until the onion is soft, 6–7 minutes. Let cool.

In a large bowl, stir together the onion mixture, spinach, chicken, sour cream, half of the mozzarella, half of the Cheddar, and the cilantro.

To assemble the enchiladas, spread 1 cup of the sauce in the prepared dish. Pour 2 cups of the sauce into a pie dish or a shallow bowl. Using tongs, dip a tortilla into the sauce. Place the tortilla on a work surface, add a few tablespoons of the chicken filling down the center, and roll up the tortilla. Place the enchilada, seam side down, in the prepared baking dish. Repeat with the remaining tortillas and filling. Drizzle all of the remaining sauce, including any left in the pie dish, evenly over the enchiladas and sprinkle with the remaining mozzarella and Cheddar. Bake until the cheese is melted and the sauce is bubbling, 30–35 minutes. Garnish with the green onions and cilantro (if using) and serve right away.

SERVES 4–6

1 tablespoon olive oil, plus more for greasing

1 recipe Enchilada Sauce (page 57)

1 lb spinach, stemmed

1 yellow onion, diced

1 clove garlic, minced

Kosher salt and freshly ground pepper

2 cups shredded cooked chicken

½ cup sour cream

1 cup shredded mozzarella cheese

½ cup shredded white Cheddar cheese

2 tablespoons chopped fresh cilantro, plus more for garnish (optional)

8–10 corn tortillas, each 6–8 inches in diameter, warmed

2 green onions, white and pale green parts, thinly sliced

Pico de Gallo & Guacamole

Use a Power Blender to whip up pico de gallo and guacamole at a moment's notice. Add margaritas (page 55) and let the party begin. The vegetables for the pico de gallo are chopped with a little water, a technique known as wet chopping (see page 12).

To make the pico de gallo, in the blender, combine the tomatoes, onion, jalapeño, and ½ cup water. With the speed on 2, pulse until the vegetables are chopped, about 15 seconds. Drain in a colander, then transfer to a bowl. Add the cilantro, lime juice, and salt to taste and toss to combine. Serve with tortilla chips.

To make the guacamole, put the onion in the blender. With the speed on 2, pulse until shredded, about 30 seconds. Scoop the avocado flesh into the blender and add the lime juice and a large pinch of salt. Blend, starting at 1 and slowly working up to 10, until the desired consistency is reached, about 30 seconds for smooth guacamole. Transfer the guacamole to a bowl and garnish with cilantro. Serve with tortilla chips.

MAKES ABOUT 2 CUPS OF EACH

For the pico de gallo

8 plum tomatoes, quartered and seeded

½ yellow onion, cut into chunks

½ jalapeño chile, halved and seeded

1 tablespoon chopped fresh cilantro

Juice of ½ lime

Kosher salt

Tortilla chips, for serving

For the guacamole

½ red onion, cut in half

4 avocados, pitted and peeled

Juice of 1 lime

Kosher salt

Chopped fresh cilantro, for garnish

Tortilla chips, for serving

Pesto Pasta Salad with Cherry Tomatoes

This recipe makes more pesto than you will need for the pasta. Leftovers are great spooned over potatoes or poached eggs, mixed with mayonnaise for sandwiches, or drizzled over steak or fish.

In the blender, combine the pine nuts, garlic, 1 teaspoon salt, and ¼ teaspoon pepper. Blend, starting at 1 and slowly working up to 10, until finely chopped, about 30 seconds. Add the basil and blend, starting at 1 and slowly working up to 10, until coarsely chopped, about 20 seconds, using the tamper as needed. With the blender running on 5, add the oil through the pour spout in a slow, steady stream and blend until smooth, 1–2 minutes. Add the lemon juice and grated cheese and blend, starting at 1 and slowly working up to 10, until incorporated, about 30 seconds. Adjust the seasoning with salt.

Meanwhile, bring a large pot of salted water to a boil over high heat. Add the pasta and cook, stirring occasionally, until al dente (tender but firm to the bite), 10–12 minutes. Drain and rinse with cold water until cool.

Transfer the pasta to a large bowl and toss with enough pesto to coat (you will not need all of it). Store the remaining pesto in an airtight container in the refrigerator for up to 1 week or in the freezer for up to 1 month. Add the tomatoes and toss to combine. Garnish with shaved cheese and pine nuts.

SERVES 4–6

¼ cup toasted pine nuts, plus more for garnish

1 large clove garlic

Kosher salt and freshly ground pepper

2½ cups packed fresh basil leaves

¾ cup extra-virgin olive oil

1 tablespoon fresh lemon juice

½ cup grated Parmesan cheese, plus shaved cheese for garnish

1 lb orecchiette

1 cup cherry tomatoes, halved

Tossed Salad with Green Goddess Dressing

This salad is packed with nutrition from a range of fresh vegetables. To make the salad a complete meal, add chickpeas, hard-boiled eggs, flaked oil-packed tuna, grilled shrimp, or shredded chicken.

To make the dressing, in the blender, combine the chives, parsley, basil, and tarragon. With the speed on 1, pulse until coarsely chopped, about 30 seconds. Add the anchovies, shallot, garlic, lemon juice, mayonnaise, buttermilk, 1 teaspoon salt, and ¼ teaspoon pepper. Blend, starting at 1 and slowly working up to 10, until smooth, about 1 minute. Adjust the seasoning with salt and pepper.

Peel, pit, and thinly slice the avocado. Thinly slice the radishes and cucumber. Cut the tomatoes in half. Trim and halve the snap peas. In a large bowl, combine the lettuce, radishes, cucumber, tomatoes, and snap peas. Toss with enough dressing to lightly coat the ingredients (you will not need all of it). Store the remaining dressing in an airtight container in the refrigerator for up to 3 days. Divide the salad among 4 plates and top with the avocado. Serve right away.

SERVES 4

For the dressing

¼ cup fresh chives

3 tablespoons fresh flat-leaf parsley

2 tablespoons fresh basil

1 tablespoon fresh tarragon

2 anchovy fillets in olive oil

1 small shallot

1 clove garlic

1 tablespoon fresh lemon juice

½ cup mayonnaise

¼ cup buttermilk

Kosher salt and freshly ground pepper

1 avocado

3 radishes

1 Persian cucumber

1 cup cherry tomatoes

1 cup sugar snap peas

8 cups mixed lettuce

Vegetable Lasagne with Roasted Tomato Sauce

Canned tomatoes are roasted to intensify their flavor in this simple yet classic lasagne. To make a heartier dish, stir 1 lb cooked ground beef or Italian sausage into the tomato sauce after blending.

Preheat the oven to 375°F. Make the roasted tomato sauce. Lightly grease a 9-by-13-inch baking dish.

Place the zucchini in a single layer on baking sheets and sprinkle with salt. Let stand for 15 minutes, then blot with paper towels. Roast until tender, 8–10 minutes. Set aside.

In a large sauté pan over medium heat, warm the oil. Add the onion and cook, stirring, until translucent, about 8 minutes. Add the garlic and cook until fragrant, about 30 seconds. Add the spinach in batches and cook until wilted, 3–4 minutes. Season with salt and pepper. Drain well.

In the blender, combine the ricotta, Parmesan, egg, ½ teaspoon salt, and ¼ teaspoon pepper. Blend, starting at 1 and slowly working up to 10, until just combined, about 20 seconds. Transfer to a bowl.

Pour ½ cup of the tomato sauce evenly on the bottom of the prepared baking dish. Cover with 4–5 noodles. Top with one-third of the ricotta mixture, half of the spinach mixture, one-third of the zucchini, and ½ cup of the tomato sauce. Sprinkle with 1 cup mozzarella. Repeat the layering 2 more times, starting with the noodles; for the last layer, omit the spinach and sprinkle with the remaining mozzarella. Cover with an oiled piece of foil. Bake until bubbly, about 30 minutes. Uncover and bake until the cheese is lightly browned, about 10 minutes longer. Let rest for 15 minutes before serving.

SERVES 8–10

1 recipe Roasted Tomato Sauce (page 57)

1 tablespoon olive oil, plus more for greasing

2 lb zucchini, cut lengthwise into planks ¼ inch thick (using a mandoline or sharp knife)

Kosher salt and freshly ground pepper

1 yellow onion, diced

2 teaspoons minced garlic

1 lb baby spinach

1 lb ricotta cheese

½ cup grated Parmesan cheese

1 large egg

15 no-boil lasagne noodles

3 cups shredded mozzarella cheese

Steak Fajitas with Avocado-Cilantro Salsa

Creamy avocado salsa elevates fajitas to an easy and delicious weeknight meal. Use flank or skirt steak for this recipe—both boast rich, beefy flavor and cook quickly on a stove-top grill pan.

To make the salsa, scoop the avocado flesh into the blender and add the oil, jalapeño, cilantro, garlic, lime juice, and a large pinch of salt. Blend, starting at 1 and slowly working up to 10, until creamy, 1–2 minutes. Adjust the seasoning with salt. Transfer the salsa to a bowl.

Preheat a stove-top grill pan over medium-high heat. Season the steak with salt and pepper. Place the steak on the pan and cook, turning once, for 8–10 minutes total for medium-rare. Transfer the steak to a cutting board, cover loosely with aluminum foil, and let rest for 5 minutes. Place the onion and bell pepper on the pan and cook, turning once, until slightly wilted and charred, about 4 minutes total. Transfer the onion and bell pepper to a plate and season with salt and pepper. Thinly slice the steak across the grain.

To assemble the fajitas, place the steak, onion, and bell pepper on the tortillas and drizzle with the avocado-cilantro salsa. Garnish with cilantro leaves and serve right away.

SERVES 6

For the salsa

1 avocado, pitted and peeled

½ cup olive oil

1 jalapeño chile

¾ cup packed fresh cilantro leaves, plus more for garnish

1 clove garlic

2 tablespoons fresh lime juice

Kosher salt and freshly ground pepper

1½ lb flank or skirt steak

1 yellow onion, thinly sliced

1 red bell pepper, seeded and thinly sliced

12 flour tortillas, warmed

Carrot-Ginger Soup

The secret to this soup's velvety texture is cooking the onion, carrots, and potato over low heat until meltingly tender and then blending everything to silky smooth perfection.

In a large, deep saucepan over medium heat, warm the oil. Add the onion, garlic, ginger, and a pinch of salt. Reduce the heat to medium-low and cook, stirring constantly, until the onion begins to soften and turn translucent, about 5 minutes. Add the carrots, potato, a pinch of salt, and a few grindings of pepper. Reduce the heat to low and cook, stirring occasionally and adding a splash of water if the vegetables start to brown or stick to the pan, until they are soft and falling apart, about 20 minutes. Add the broth, raise the heat to medium-low, and cook until the flavors deepen, about 20 minutes longer.

Transfer the soup to the blender. Blend, starting at 1 and slowly working up to 10, until smooth, 2–3 minutes. Add more broth, water, or cream (if using) to reach the desired consistency. Adjust the seasoning with salt and pepper.

Pour the soup into bowls and garnish with crème fraîche, almonds, mint, and cilantro (if using). Serve warm.

SERVES 4

2 tablespoons olive oil

1 yellow onion, thinly sliced

2 cloves garlic, thinly sliced

2-inch piece fresh ginger, peeled and thinly sliced

Kosher salt and freshly ground pepper

1 lb carrots (3 or 4 large carrots), peeled and cut into 1-inch pieces

1 Yukon gold potato, peeled and cut into 1-inch pieces

3 cups chicken or vegetable broth or water, plus more as needed

2 tablespoons heavy cream (optional)

Crème fraîche, toasted almonds, and fresh mint and cilantro leaves, for garnish (optional)

Try different toppings, such as sauerkraut, kimchi, pickled red onions, or sliced jalapeños.

Pulled Pork Sliders with Coleslaw

Pulled pork sandwiches have never been easier. Blend a cooking liquid for the pork that later doubles as a delicious barbecue sauce for the sandwiches. Top with sweet-and-sour coleslaw for bright crunch.

In the blender, combine the vinegar, ketchup, brown sugar, garlic, onion, salt, mustard, paprika, cayenne, and ½ cup water. Blend, starting at 1 and slowly working up to 10, until well combined, about 30 seconds.

If using a Dutch oven, preheat the oven to 350°F.

In a 5-quart Dutch oven or in the stove top–safe insert of a slow cooker over medium-high heat, warm the oil. Brown the pork shoulder on all sides, 7–9 minutes total. Transfer to a plate. Pour out any rendered fat and return the pork to the pot or insert. Add the vinegar mixture.

If using a Dutch oven, cover, transfer to the oven, and cook until the pork is tender and pulls apart easily, 4–6 hours. If using a slow cooker, transfer the insert to the slow-cooker base, cover, and cook on high according to the manufacturer's instructions until the pork is tender and pulls apart easily, 5–6 hours. Make the coleslaw.

Transfer the pork to a large bowl. When cool enough to handle, shred the meat with 2 forks, discarding any large pieces of fat. Place the Dutch oven or slow-cooker insert with the cooking liquid on the stovetop over medium-high heat. Simmer until the liquid thickens and is reduced by half, 8–10 minutes. Toss the pork with some of the sauce.

Serve the pork on the buns, topped with more sauce and the coleslaw.

SERVES 4–6

1½ cups cider vinegar

½ cup tomato ketchup

⅓ cup firmly packed light brown sugar

4 cloves garlic

1 onion

2 teaspoons kosher salt

3 tablespoons dry mustard

2 tablespoons paprika

Pinch of cayenne pepper

2 tablespoons canola oil

2½ lb boneless pork shoulder

1 recipe Coleslaw (page 58)

8–10 mini hamburger buns, toasted

Cauliflower-Kale Soup with Crispy Kale Topping

This silky soup gets depth of flavor from roasted cauliflower, while kale lends a beautiful green hue. Crispy kale and pine nuts add satisfying crunch.

Preheat the oven to 450°F. In a large bowl, toss together the cauliflower and 2 tablespoons of the oil and season with salt and pepper. Transfer to a baking sheet. Roast, stirring occasionally, until the cauliflower is tender and the edges are browned and crisp, about 22 minutes. Reduce the oven temperature to 300°F.

In a bowl, toss together half of the kale and 1 tablespoon of the oil, and season with salt. Transfer to a baking sheet. Roast, stirring once halfway through, until the kale is crispy, 26–28 minutes. Set aside.

Meanwhile, in a Dutch oven over medium heat, warm the remaining 2 tablespoons oil. Add the onion and celery and cook, stirring occasionally, until tender, about 8 minutes. Add the garlic and cook, stirring constantly, for 1 minute. Season with salt and pepper. Add the cauliflower and broth, raise the heat to medium-high, and bring to a simmer. Reduce the heat to medium-low, cover, and cook for 10 minutes. Stir in the remaining kale, increase the heat to medium, and cook, uncovered, for 10 minutes.

Working in batches, transfer the soup to the blender. Blend, starting at 1 and slowly working up to 10, until smooth, 1–2 minutes. Return the soup to the pot and adjust the seasoning with salt and pepper.

Ladle the soup into bowls and garnish with the crispy kale and pine nuts. Serve warm.

SERVES 6–8

1 large head cauliflower, trimmed and cut into florets

5 tablespoons olive oil

Kosher salt and freshly ground pepper

1 large bunch Tuscan kale, stemmed and leaves torn into 1-inch pieces

1 yellow onion, diced

2 ribs celery, diced

3 cloves garlic, minced

7 cups chicken or vegetable broth

1/3 cup pine nuts, toasted, for garnish

Experiment with other greens such as Swiss chard or spinach.

Make the glaze up to 2 days ahead of time and store in the refrigerator. Brush it onto the salmon just before broiling.

Sweet & Spicy
Sriracha-Glazed Salmon

Sweet and spicy, this Sriracha-glazed salmon is a crowd-pleaser and fit for a dinner party since it comes together in minutes. Adjust the amount of Sriracha depending on the desired level of heat.

Preheat the broiler. Line a baking sheet with aluminum foil.

In the blender, combine the soy sauce, honey, brown sugar, hoisin sauce, Sriracha, ginger, garlic, and lime juice. Blend, starting at 1 and slowly working up to 10, until the garlic and ginger are puréed, about 30 seconds.

Pour the soy sauce mixture into a small saucepan. Place over medium-high heat and simmer, stirring occasionally, until the mixture is reduced by half and forms a glaze, 5–7 minutes.

Place the salmon on the prepared baking sheet and pour the glaze over the fish. Broil until the salmon is just cooked through, 6–8 minutes. Garnish with green onion and cilantro and serve right away.

SERVES 4

⅓ cup soy sauce

2 tablespoons honey

2 tablespoons firmly packed light brown sugar

1 tablespoon hoisin sauce

2 teaspoons Sriracha, or to taste

1-inch piece fresh ginger, peeled

2 cloves garlic

Juice of 1 lime

4 salmon fillets, 6 oz each

Sliced green onion and fresh cilantro leaves, for garnish

Chicken Skewers with Herbed Balsamic Marinade

A zingy marinade with herbs and sweet-tart balsamic vinegar gives these chicken skewers tons of flavor with little effort. Double the recipe and serve leftovers with a salad or tucked into a pita sandwich.

If using wooden skewers, soak 4 skewers in water for about 30 minutes, then drain.

To make the marinade, in the blender, combine the oil, vinegar, 2 teaspoons salt, the mustard, red pepper flakes, parsley, thyme, garlic, and shallot. Blend, starting at 1 and slowly working up to 10, until the garlic and shallot are finely chopped and the mixture is emulsified, about 1 minute.

Pour the marinade into a lock-top plastic bag, add the chicken and bell pepper, and seal the bag. Refrigerate for 1 hour.

Prepare a hot fire in a charcoal or gas grill.

Remove the chicken and bell pepper from the marinade and thread onto 4 metal or wooden skewers, alternating the pieces and dividing them evenly. Arrange the skewers on the grill and cook, turning occasionally, until the chicken is lightly charred and cooked through, about 20 minutes.

Transfer the skewers to a serving platter and serve.

SERVES 2

For the marinade

½ cup olive oil

2 tablespoons balsamic vinegar

Kosher salt

1 teaspoon Dijon mustard

¼ teaspoon red pepper flakes

¼ cup packed fresh flat-leaf parsley leaves

1 teaspoon fresh thyme leaves

1 clove garlic

1 shallot

1 lb skinless, boneless chicken thighs, cut into 1-inch pieces

1 red bell pepper, seeded and cut into 1-inch pieces

Pork Tenderloin with Plum Chutney

Make the marinade and chutney a day or two in advance, then whip up this all-star dinner in no time! Finely dice the ingredients for a classic look or use the blender to create a delicious sauce.

To make the marinade, in the blender, combine the vinegar, ⅓ cup oil, soy sauce, honey, thyme, and garlic. Blend, starting at 1 and slowly working up to 10, until well combined, about 30 seconds. Pour the marinade into a lock-top plastic bag, add the pork tenderloin, and seal the bag. Refrigerate for at least 2 hours or up to overnight. Wash and dry the blender container. Make the plum chutney.

To make the topping, in the blender, combine the bread, oil, thyme, rosemary, 1 tablespoon salt, and 1 tablespoon pepper. With the speed on 3, pulse until fine crumbs form, about 1 minute. Set aside.

Preheat the oven to 375°F. Remove the pork from the marinade and let stand at room temperature for 15 minutes. In a large ovenproof frying pan over medium-high heat, warm the remaining 2 tablespoons oil. Add the pork and cook until well browned, 3–4 minutes per side. Off the heat, cover the top of the pork with the bread crumb topping.

Transfer the pan to the oven and roast until an instant-read thermometer inserted into the center of the pork registers 145°F, 10–20 minutes. Transfer the pork to a cutting board, cover loosely with aluminum foil, and let rest for 5–10 minutes. Cut into ½-inch slices and serve warm with the plum chutney.

SERVES 4–6

For the marinade and pork

⅔ cup sherry vinegar

⅓ cup plus 2 tablespoons extra-virgin olive oil

2 tablespoons soy sauce

1 tablespoon honey

2 tablespoons thyme

4 cloves garlic

2 lb pork tenderloin

1 recipe Plum Chutney (page 59)

For the bread crumb topping

2 slices bread, lightly toasted

1 tablespoon extra-virgin olive oil

1 tablespoon fresh thyme

1 tablespoon fresh chopped rosemary

Kosher salt and freshly ground pepper

Mac & Cheese

Making mac and cheese is a snap with the help of a Power Blender, which shreds the cheese and blends the béchamel sauce. Use your favorite dried short pasta in this classic dish.

Preheat the oven to 375°F.

Bring a large pot of salted water to a boil over high heat. Add the pasta and cook, stirring occasionally, until not quite al dente (tender but firm to the bite), about 2 minutes less than the package instructions. Drain and transfer to a large bowl.

Put the Cheddar in the blender. Blend, starting at 1 and slowly working up to 10, until shredded, about 30 seconds. Transfer to a bowl. Wash and dry the blender container.

In the blender, combine the butter, flour, milk, and cream. Blend, starting at 1 and slowly working up to 10, until heavy steam comes out of the blender and the mixture is warm, 5–8 minutes. Add half of the Cheddar, the nutmeg, and large pinch each of salt and pepper. Blend, starting at 1 and slowly working up to 10, until combined, about 30 seconds.

Pour the sauce over the pasta, add the remaining Cheddar, and stir well. Transfer to a 3-quart shallow baking dish or large baking dish with a similar capacity. Top with the Parmesan and panko. Bake until the top is lightly browned and the sauce is bubbly, 15–20 minutes. Let stand for 5 minutes before serving.

SERVES 4–6

Kosher salt and freshly ground pepper

1 lb dried short pasta, such as straccetti or campanelle

4 cups cubed sharp yellow Cheddar cheese

4 tablespoons unsalted butter

¼ cup all-purpose flour

2 cups whole milk

1 cup heavy cream

¼ teaspoon ground nutmeg

¼ cup grated Parmesan or pecorino cheese

¼ cup panko bread crumbs

Strawberry Sorbet & Strawberry Frozen Yogurt

This recipe gives you the option of making either a refreshing sorbet or creamy frozen yogurt. In place of the strawberries, feel free to swap in your favorite fresh or frozen berries such as raspberries or blueberries.

To make the strawberry sorbet, in the blender, combine the strawberries, sugar, lemon zest, lemon juice, and ½ teaspoon salt. Blend, starting at 1 and slowly working up to 10, until completely combined, about 1 minute. Transfer to a freezer-safe container, cover, and freeze until firm, at least 4 hours or up to 2 weeks.

To make the strawberry frozen yogurt, in the blender, combine the strawberries, sugar, lemon zest, lemon juice, and ½ teaspoon salt. Blend, starting at 1 and slowly working up to 10, until completely combined, about 1 minute. Add the yogurt and blend, starting at 1 and slowly working up to 10, until combined, about 15 seconds. Transfer to a freezer-safe container, cover, and freeze until firm, at least 4 hours or up to 2 weeks.

MAKES 1 QUART SORBET OR 1½ QUARTS YOGURT

For the strawberry sorbet

4 cups fresh strawberries (about 1½ lb), hulled

¾ cup sugar

Zest and juice of 1 lemon

Kosher salt

For the strawberry frozen yogurt

4 cups fresh strawberries (about 1½ lb), hulled

¾ cup sugar

Zest and juice of 1 lemon

Kosher salt

1½ cups plain full-fat Greek yogurt

Bittersweet Chocolate Pudding

This incredibly rich chocolate pudding is a grown-up take on a childhood favorite. For a more sophisticated dessert, top with whipped cream and sea salt flakes.

Put the chocolate in the blender. Set aside. In a heatproof large bowl, whisk together the sugar, cornstarch, cocoa powder, and a pinch of kosher salt. In a small bowl, briefly whisk together the egg yolks and cream. Pour over the sugar mixture and whisk to combine. Set aside.

In a saucepan over medium-high heat, bring the milk to a simmer, then remove from the heat and quickly stir about ¼ cup of the milk into the egg mixture. Continue adding the hot milk ¼ cup at a time, stirring constantly. When all of the milk has been added, pour the mixture back into the same pan. Place over low heat and cook, whisking constantly and scraping the bottom of the pan to ensure even cooking, until thickened, about 3 minutes.

Press the milk mixture through a fine-mesh sieve set over the blender. Let stand for a few minutes to allow the chocolate to melt. Remove the plug from the lid so steam can escape. Blend, starting at 1 and slowly working up to 10, until smooth, 1–2 minutes. Add the vanilla and pulse to combine.

Divide the chocolate mixture among eight 6-oz ramekins, jars, or small bowls and refrigerate until chilled, at least 1 hour or up to 2 days. Just before serving, top the pudding with whipped cream and sea salt flakes, if using.

SERVES 8

4 oz bittersweet chocolate, broken into large pieces

¾ cup sugar

¼ cup cornstarch

3 tablespoons unsweetened cocoa powder

Kosher salt

3 large egg yolks

½ cup heavy cream

2 cups whole milk

2 teaspoons vanilla extract

Whipped cream (page 16) and sea salt flakes, for garnish (optional)

Sea salt flakes enhance the chocolate flavor of this bittersweet pudding.

Cheesecake with Sour Cream Topping

Here, a creamy, vanilla-flecked filling is layered between a salty-sweet graham cracker crust and a tangy topping. Top with berries or stone fruit in summer or roasted figs, apples, or pears during the cooler months.

Make the graham cracker crust. Place 2 racks in the lower half of the oven and preheat to 325°F. Fill a shallow roasting pan with water and place on the bottom rack.

To make the filling, in the blender, combine the cream cheese, sour cream, and sugar. Blend, starting at 1 and slowly working up to 10, until smooth, about 1 minute. Add the eggs and blend, starting at 1 and slowly working up to 10, until completely incorporated, about 30 seconds. Add the lemon juice, vanilla extract, and vanilla bean seeds and blend, starting at 1 and slowly working up to 10, until distributed, about 30 seconds. Pour the filling into the crust.

Bake until the edges are set and the center jiggles just slightly, 65–80 minutes. Begin checking for doneness after 65 minutes. If the top is browning too quickly, tent with foil. Let cool to room temperature on a wire rack, then refrigerate until cold, at least 4 hours or up to 4 days.

To make the sour cream topping, in a bowl, whisk together the sour cream and confectioners' sugar until smooth. Whisk in the vanilla. Refrigerate until ready to use.

To serve, run a knife around the edge of the pan. Release the pan sides and transfer the cheesecake to a serving platter. Spread the sour cream topping over the top. Refrigerate for 30 minutes before serving.

SERVES 12–16

1 recipe Graham Cracker Crust (page 56)

For the filling

1½ lb cream cheese, at room temperature

1 cup sour cream

1 cup sugar

3 large eggs

1 tablespoon fresh lemon juice

1 teaspoon vanilla extract

1 vanilla bean, split and seeds scraped

For the sour cream topping

1 cup sour cream

¼ cup confectioners' sugar, sifted

½ teaspoon vanilla extract

Watermelon-Mint Granita

For an elegant dessert, layer this granita over frozen yogurt and garnish with fresh mint leaves. And for a summer treat, pour your favorite tequila or prosecco over a scoop to make a delicious cocktail.

In the blender, combine the watermelon and simple syrup. Blend, starting at 1 and slowly working up to 10, until puréed, 1–2 sminutes. Add the mint and lime juice. Blend, starting at 1 and slowly working up to 10, until combined, about 10 seconds. Taste and add more simple syrup, as needed.

Pour the watermelon mixture into a 9-by-5-inch loaf pan. Freeze until solid, at least 8 hours or up to overnight.

When completely frozen, use a fork to scrape the granita into flakes and serve. Store in the freezer for up to 2 weeks.

MAKES ABOUT 1 QUART

1½ lb roughly cubed or sliced seedless watermelon (from a 3–3½-lb watermelon)

¼ cup Simple Syrup (see recipe), plus more as needed

12 fresh mint leaves

1 tablespoon fresh lime juice

Simple Syrup

In a saucepan, combine equal parts sugar and water and stir to dissolve the sugar. Place over high heat and bring to a boil. Remove from the heat and let cool to room temperature. Store in an airtight container in the refrigerator for up to 1 month.

Frozen Margaritas

Pitcher perfect! Blend up this frozen version of the classic margarita or try one of our refreshing twists. Serve with homemade guacamole (page 29), and let the fiesta begin.

In the blender, combine the tequila, lime juice, simple syrup, triple sec (if using), and 4 cups of the ice. Blend, starting at 1 and slowly working up to 10, until the ice is crushed, about 1 minute. Add more ice as needed to reach the desired slushy consistency.

Pour a layer of salt on a small plate. Moisten the rims of 4 glasses with lime wedges, then dip the rims into the salt. Pour the margaritas into the glasses and garnish with lime wedges.

Variations

Strawberry-Basil Margarita: Add 2 cups frozen strawberries and ½ cup fresh basil leaves when blending.

Cucumber-Mint Margarita: Add 1 cup peeled, seeded, and chopped cucumber and ½ cup fresh mint leaves when blending. Garnish with sliced cucumber and whole mint leaves.

Coconut-Lime Margarita: Add 1 can (15 fl oz) coconut cream when blending. Stir grated lime zest into the coarse salt before dipping the rims of the glasses.

Ginger-Peach Margarita: Add 1 cup frozen peaches, 1 cup ginger ale, and 1 tablespoon grated fresh ginger when blending. Garnish with a lime wedge or a fresh peach slice.

SERVES 4

1 cup tequila

½ cup fresh lime juice

½ cup Simple Syrup (page 54)

½ cup triple sec or Cointreau (optional)

4–8 cups ice cubes

Coarse salt and lime wedges, for garnish

Graham Cracker Crust

Preheat the oven to 350°F. Butter the bottom and sides of a 9-by-3-inch springform pan.

In the blender, combine the graham crackers, sugar, and salt. Blend, starting at 1 and slowly working up to 10, until fine crumbs form, about 30 seconds. Drizzle in the melted butter and blend, starting at 1 and slowly working up to 10, until the mixture resembles wet sand, about 30 seconds. Press into the prepared pan. Bake until golden brown, about 10 minutes. Let cool on a wire rack before filling.

MAKES ONE 9-INCH CRUST

5 tablespoons unsalted butter, melted, plus more for greasing

14 honey graham crackers, broken in half

1 tablespoon sugar

Pinch of kosher salt

Berry Compote

In a saucepan, combine the berries, sugar, lemon zest, and lemon juice. Place over medium heat and cook, stirring occasionally, until the sugar is dissolved and the mixture thickens, about 15 minutes. Stir in the butter. For a smoother sauce, transfer the compote to the blender and blend, starting at 1 and slowly working up to 10, until smooth, about 30 seconds. Serve the compote warm or store in an airtight container in the refrigerator for up to 1 week; gently reheat before serving.

MAKES ABOUT 2 CUPS

3 cups fresh or frozen mixed berries, such as blueberries, strawberries, or blackberries

½ cup sugar

Zest and juice of 1 lemon

2 tablespoons unsalted butter

Roasted Tomato Sauce

Preheat the oven to 500°F. Place the tomatoes, cut side up, on an aluminum foil–lined baking sheet. Drizzle with 2 tablespoons of the oil. Roast, turning once, until beginning to wilt, about 15 minutes.

In the blender, combine the tomatoes and the remaining 2 tablespoons oil. Blend, starting at 1 and slowly working up to 10, until slightly chunky, about 10 seconds, using the tamper as needed. Add the red pepper flakes and basil. With the speed on 2, pulse until combined, about 30 seconds. Season with salt and black pepper. Transfer to a bowl. Use right away or store in an airtight container in the refrigerator for up to 5 days.

MAKES ABOUT 4 CUPS

2 cans (28 oz each) whole tomatoes, drained and halved

4 tablespoons olive oil

¼ teaspoon red pepper flakes

¼ cup chopped fresh basil

Kosher salt and freshly ground black pepper

Enchilada Sauce

In the blender, combine the onion, bell pepper, jalapeño, garlic, cumin, broth, tomatoes with their juices, chipotle chile, and a large pinch of salt. Blend, starting at 1 and slowly working up to 10, until smooth, 1–2 minutes.

Pour the tomato mixture into a saucepan. Place over medium-high heat and simmer, stirring occasionally, until reduced by half, about 15 minutes. Adjust the seasoning with salt. Let cool. Use right away or store in an airtight container for up to 5 days.

MAKES ABOUT 3 CUPS

1 yellow onion, quartered

1 green bell pepper, seeded and quartered

1 jalapeño chile

2 cloves garlic

1 tablespoon ground cumin

2 cups chicken broth

1 can (28 oz) whole tomatoes with juices

1 chipotle chile in adobo

Kosher salt

Honey Butter

In the blender, combine the butter, honey, and salt. With the speed on 4, blend until light and fluffy, 2–3 minutes, using the tamper as needed to push down the ingredients. Use right away or store in an airtight container in the refrigerator for up to 5 days.

MAKES ABOUT 1 CUP

1 cup unsalted butter, at room temperature

¼ cup honey

1 teaspoon sea salt flakes

Coleslaw

In the blender, combine the carrots, cabbage, and ½ cup water. With the speed on 1 or 2, pulse until the vegetables are shredded, 7–9 pulses. Drain in a colander, then transfer to a bowl.

To make the dressing, in a small bowl, whisk together the vinegar, oil, sugar, garlic, mustard, celery seeds, and salt. Pour the dressing over the cabbage mixture and toss together. Let the coleslaw stand at room temperature for 15 minutes before serving. The coleslaw can be stored in an airtight container in the refrigerator for up to 2 days.

MAKES ABOUT 3 CUPS

2 carrots, peeled and cut into 2-inch pieces

¼ green cabbage, cored and cut into large pieces

¼ red cabbage, cored and cut into large pieces

For the dressing

½ cup white wine vinegar

2 tablespoons canola oil

¼ cup sugar

1 clove garlic, minced

2 tablespoons whole-grain mustard

1 teaspoon celery seeds

Pinch of kosher salt

Streusel

Put the pecans in the blender. With the speed on 1 or 2, pulse a few times until coarsely chopped. In a bowl, whisk together the flour, sugar, and salt, then add the pecans. Drizzle in the melted butter and stir until well incorporated. The streusel should be clumpy. Freeze for at least 10 minutes before using.

MAKES ABOUT 1 CUP

½ cup toasted pecans

¼ cup all-purpose flour

¼ cup sugar

Pinch of kosher salt

3 tablespoons unsalted butter, melted

Plum Chutney

In the blender, combine the shallot, garlic, and plums. With the speed on 1, pulse until coarsely chopped, about 30 seconds.

In a frying pan over medium heat, warm the oil. Add the blended plum mixture and salt and cook, stirring frequently, until the shallot is translucent and the garlic is fragrant, about 3 minutes. Add the brown sugar, vinegar, mustard seeds (if using), and red pepper flakes (if using). Cook, stirring frequently, until the fruit is tender and the liquid has thickened, about 10 minutes. Serve warm or store in an airtight container in the refrigerator for up to 2 days; gently reheat before serving.

MAKES ABOUT 1 CUP

1 shallot

2 cloves garlic

4 plums, pitted

1 tablespoon extra-virgin olive oil

Pinch of kosher salt

⅓ cup firmly packed light brown sugar

⅓ cup sherry vinegar

2 tablespoons yellow mustard seeds (optional)

1 tablespoon red pepper flakes (optional)

Index

THE PERFECT BLENDING COOKBOOK

Conceived and produced by Weldon Owen, Inc.
In collaboration with Williams-Sonoma, Inc.
3250 Van Ness Avenue, San Francisco, CA 94109

A WELDON OWEN PRODUCTION
1045 Sansome Street, Suite 100
San Francisco, CA 94111
www.weldonowen.com

Copyright © 2015 Weldon Owen, Inc.
and Williams-Sonoma, Inc.
All rights reserved, including the right of
reproduction in whole or in part in any form.

Printed in the United States by Worzalla

First printed in 2015
10 9 8 7 6 5 4 3 2 1

Library of Congress Cataloging-in-Publication
data is available.

ISBN 13: 978-1-68188-023-5
ISBN 10: 1-68188-023-7

WELDON OWEN, INC.
President & Publisher Roger Shaw
SVP, Sales & Marketing Amy Kaneko
Finance Manager Philip Paulick

Associate Publisher Amy Marr
Associate Editor Emma Rudolph

Creative Director Kelly Booth
Art Director Marisa Kwek
Associate Art Director Lisa Berman
Senior Production Designer Rachel Lopez Metzger

Production Director Chris Hemesath
Associate Production Director Michelle Duggan
Production Manager Michelle Woo

Photographer Maren Caruso
Food Stylist Erin Quon
Prop Stylist Laura Cook

Weldon Owen is a division of **BONNIER**

ACKNOWLEDGMENTS

Weldon Owen wishes to thank the following people for their generous support in
producing this book: Kris Balloun, Tina Dang, Alma Espinola, Sean Franzen, Gloria Geller,
Kim Laidlaw, and Elizabeth Parson.

Vitamix is a registered trademark of Vita-Mix Corporation.